AWAKEN, BELLS FALLING

AWAKEN, BELLS FALLING

Poems 1959–1967 by

LEWIS TURCO

Missouri Literary Frontiers Series Number 4

UNIVERSITY OF MISSOURI PRESS

COLUMBIA • MISSOURI

for John Brinnin and Don Justice

If it is true that
"the sea worm is a decorated flute
that pipes in the most ancient mode" —
and if it is true, too, that
"the salt content of mammalian blood
is exactly equivalent
to the salinity of the oceans
at the time life emerged onto the land";

and if it is true
that "man is the only mammal with a
capacity for song," well, then,
that explains why the baroque
worm swims in our veins, piping, and why
we dance to his measure inch by
equivocal inch. And it explains why
this song, even as it explains nothing.

CONTENTS

ACKNOWLEDGMENTS

Some of these poems have previously appeared in the following periodicals, to the editors and publishers of which the author owes thanks and acknowledgment for permission to reprint: *Antioch Review, Approach, Carleton Miscellany, Carolina Quarterly, Choice, Commonweal, Literary Review, Massachusetts Review, The Mid-Century, Minnesota Review, A New England Review, Northwest Review, A Nosegay in Black, Paris Review, Poetry Northwest, Prairie Schooner, Premiere, The Quest, Saturday Review, Tri-Quarterly, University Review, Voices, Wormwood Review,* and *Yankee.*

"November 22, 1963," "Awaken, Bells Falling," and "House and Shutter" were originally published in *Poetry* and copyrighted, respectively, in 1964, 1964, and 1960 by the Modern Poetry Association.

"An Ordinary Evening in Cleveland" appeared originally in *The New Yorker.*

"The Old Professor and the Sphinx" was originally published in *Northwest Review* and was reprinted in *The Best Poems of 1965: The Borestone Mountain Poetry Awards, 1966.*

Lines two and three of the dedicatory poem are quoted from the poem "Argonauts" by Joel Sloman in *Virgil's Machines,* copyright 1966 by Joel Sloman and reprinted by permission of the publisher, W. W. Norton & Company, Inc.

The author owes expression of his gratitude as well to Mr. Brian Macdonald, Director of the Harkness Ballet, who made a dance, "While the Spider Slept," of the poem "November 22, 1963." No less gratitude to the members of the Royal Swedish Ballet and the Royal Winnipeg Ballet who have performed the work in Europe and North America.

THE TOWNSFOLK

There is, first, the road,
which goes nowhere out of
nowhere endlessly. And beside
it, beside the road, grass
and flowers growing, some trees,

leaves covered with dust.
A barn stands caught in a
twist of the road, paint peeling in
the insensible sun.
Somewhere a dove mourns under

eaves. A phoebe calls
out the season crisply,
and the townsfolk move out of nowhere, walking, going no-
where with birdcalls and flowers.

In a White Direction
for Sal

I have come, cousin,
to wish you good night. The hubs
of your eyes make no worlds careen now;
the spokes of shadow are bent

and broken beneath
your lashes. What a wish to
wish you: good night, with its circular
lie. You stretch beneath your sheets,

ridged and humped like some
winter terrain. No person's
sight will travel you again. It is
here we must stop now, in this

blind alley of flesh.
The mind cannot compass you.
My breath stops and starts in its tunnel,
the permanent wind moving

in sentient hollows;
it is a vague piston in
my veins pushing red motion through curbs
time has constructed. But you,

cousin. I wish you
good night. There shall be no maps
now, no turns. Direction comes back to
this:
Darkness on winter roads.

LOST GIRL WITH DOG

Improbably fair, picture girl, your hair
settled like a mist above the closed lids of your eyes,
you lie in the warm snow, and the collie howls

quietly into the night. You are tacked
four square to the wall. A pattern of slatternly vines
and rose blossoms weaves wearily behind and

about you. You are a gateway in the
wallpaper, and she searches you from time to time. *This
is how it might have been with me,* she thinks. *I,*

too, might have made such a lovely painting.
She nods and turns away. You are left in suspension.
The blizzard spills on your still form like petals.

What if the dog should move his hushed tail and go
yelping into sharp darkness for help? Little girl lost
in the woods of sleep, what if that lone star

came sweeping with raging feathers, nails raking
out of the glass to scatter your drab dream and hers? She
leans and settles, neutral and thick, in corners

of the dark house. The pattern of her dress is
dry leaves and brown blossoms. Her steps upon the carpet
drop like flakes. She passes and repasses

you and your collie, stopping now and then to
lodge her heavy eyes in cotton worlds of snow. She nods
and goes pressing back into brown patterns.

LETTER TO W.D.S.

Christ, you made me sad
with your love tunes gone awry,
the bitter root twining mossily
among the pages of a songsheet tossed to

wind down the wind and
moulder in a lost cranny
of some meadow. I'm not used to loss,
though aware of it, as one is aware of

cancer. A woman
I knew, wrinkled like blown snow,
died of a wild part of herself which
ravened its own life. Her children, grown to seed

themselves, kept locks on
their tongues, but their hearts' faceless
prisoner snarled at the world behind
portcullises of eyes. Like those striped lines of

yours, that scourge of ink
and pillory of paper.
Why did you flay yourself there, in the
marketplace? Was it because sorrow shown is

simpler than covert
loneliness? All of us are
alone. The world we blow through is cold.
Snow fetters our sorrow. Still we flute and fife.

MICE IN THE SUNDAY WALLS

The grey rain, like mice scurrying about the house,
nibbles the edges of a moldy afternoon.
Sunday's trap is set for us to trigger.
The doorbell. The door. The whole hall hungry,
its yellow stairs snapping at our laces; the old
    lady mewing in the parlor, arching
her aching back — O! The same old tom in the same

    armchair rising, dragging his sagging tail
    over the carpet to welcome us back.
The cool cat gone, off in his Olds down the alley,
the motor purring convertibly; seduction
    sloshing contentiously in the gas tank:
gone, man, gone. Sunday rustles in the walls. We four
    sit lapping the skim of our duty call.

                *   *   *   *   *   *

This is the way the old folks seem at last. Death sprawls
on the couch to doze an age. But metaphor will
    not suffice to crystallize aversion;
    nor simile, our compassion. There is
nowhere to go, nothing to see, little to do
    here in childhood's hall of mirrors. Backward
and forward, reflected in each-other's vision,

    distorted images of our common
    love separate, then merge, then fade and fail.
We talk. Quietly at first, for fear of shadows.
Days, like mice, have overgenerated. They now
    outnumber the old folks' hungers. Soon we
will leave, and no one will reflect on anyone
    for very long. Nor too deeply. Nor far.

Lines for Mr. Stevenson

Here, music
is martial. Wars and their rumors
echo among these cold walls. I recall
one who kept

the beat with
his shoe — the cadence of its heel
used a desk in a way I could not have
dreamed. A world

speaks in so
many tongues, it is difficult
to hear truth whispering out of Babel.
Even so,

one must try.
At least, I believe so, and one
will be chastised for daring to believe:
the single

conviction
must stand against the myrmidons
of truism and rumor — must prevail
at last, or

there is no
hope. But flesh tires; the mind will
wear it out if the drums don't wear it down.
Even the

warrior
need not fight forever. Where are
the young men? There is music I should like
to hear; *for*

a while, I
would just like to sit in the shade
with a glass of wine in my hands, and watch
people dance.

HE WHO FEEDS PIGEONS

I have not been here long.
I sit in the park and feed the pigeons.
In my pocket there are crumbs and catches,
and an old, broken chess piece
left over from some forgotten game.
I no longer play with pawns and kings,

nor do I have to do with bishops —
they are all dead men. Instead, the world
is an aerie filled with wings.
If you should ask me why I venerate
the grass and the birds and playing children
above all other things,

I would not tell you. There are things no man
can tell, and none understand unless
he is willing to bring
in his pockets the remnants of song, crusts,
winters of memory, and drop them
in handfuls, thus, on the ground.

Weeping, I write this: You are dead. The dark
animal of the heart, the beast that bides
stilly in its web of flesh, has stolen
flight again out of the air. What is there
to say? That I wish we were gods? That the
mind of man were equal to his lusts? It
is not — not yet. You were a man, but more:
you were an idea dreamt in a sweet
hour while the spider slept. We make our
web: its habitant makes greatness of its
prey. We are ourselves victim and victor.
You were and are ourselves. In killing you
we murder an emblem of what we strive
to be: not men, but Man. In mourning you,
good Man, we grieve for what we are, not what
we may become.
                Sleep, my heart. We will try
once more. Sleep, sleep, John. We will try again.

My Country Wife

My country wife bends to rinse. Her skirt is
    unwrinkled. Its print of flowers rounds
out her womb like the rug of violets
    that mounds or dimples the chapel
burying ground. She would be grotesque where
    hydrants irrigate gutters.

Here, she is a sleight of the moon; the sound
    a mole makes. She bends and carries. She
cooks and smiles her meals down my throat. I need
    no teeth. She has done what the bee
does to clover. The sun moves around. She
    stays and stays. She sweeps and cooks.

My Wife of the Town

The stairs are teeth that chew her heels.
She grows shorter each day. The child
tears her with nails and with cries. I cannot hear
        the night sounds that burrow
in the sheets, unwinding her like thread
        onto the winter boards.

She moves in the closets mewling
among the garments as though she
were a sleeve looking for its coat. Where are they,
        those sheep days, wool days, days
fleeced from green time and woven to wear?
        A black rat chews her heels.

Who are you, he asked me
curiously, without conceit, yet
— I could feel it, but I cannot say it
exactly — holding something back,
keeping it out of his eyes,

out of his smile. He stood still, holding
out his hand, like a roadmap we were to
travel together openly.
His eyes were brown, warm enough,
but with a heat that could

never fuse: the mesa of his nose was
much too high for them to surmount . . . ,
poor lovers. Imagine, not
ever to cross, only
to wander side by side and worship

from afar, as it is done in
penny novels. His lips: one
was thin, the other plump:
a miser bedding his jolly wife.
Under the mattress a chin was hiding.

It was neither sturdy nor
frail — a compromise in
a compromising situation.
But above all, a brown heath spread its hay
over redness and ruddiness, and

yet, though he stood smiling
openly, there was that about him
which I could not fathom. *No, who are you,*
I asked, smiling warmly into
his face, thrusting my hand far

as it would go into the shallow glass.

NARCISSUS TO HIS FLESHLY SHADE

I want her to be what I need
her to be, *i.e.*, a mirror for my
want. There is no man but owns his own soul.
    His lack lies in the catalyst.
Surmise it or not, what she cannot know
    is what image she replaces,

    or why the moon's in her lashes
and in mine. The moon is one mirror of
a world, but purer for perspective, for
    distance. Our man knows himself too
well for glassless love. You are too near, dear
    shade! Fall back on deeper shallows.

AN OLD ACQUAINTANCE

As we stand talking, his eye
drops out. I am amazed.
His socket looks funny.
It's a nice day, I say.
His scalp is scattered on the

carpet. What's the matter with
your nose, I ask — but it
is too late. He laughs. His
teeth hit something on their
way down. I must be getting

on, I suggest. But I am
too slow to catch his ear.
Can't you say something, I
inquire: he opens his
mouth to show me. That's too bad,

I say, but he shakes his head
too hard. I try looking
into his mind, but he
is thinking of nothing.
A spider is spinning her

web in a white cave. It is
awkward. Well, it's getting
late, I say. The spider
has caught something. I smile
at him; he stands there grinning.

A continuous curtain, the
mist rises and rises on no cue at all. Here
lies the farm on bottomland. Marshmallow
blooms blossom like cathedrals in
the mist. The stage is dark. Loam lies down with stagnant

water to breed vapors and moss.
It is silent here, for the farmhouse wants to rot.
By night it breathes steam from broken garrets.
In the cellar, walls distill (drop
by drop by drop) the juices of a luminous

cancer, and the foundations search
deeper for fundament. Rust has pilfered the plow;
the weight of the sky has scuttled the barn;
the willow roots in the cistern.
Bottomland lets no marker stand for long: no stone

shows by the sycamore tree, nor
footway runs the dooryard's course. Henbane roosts in the
parlor chair. A loveseat drowses like an
old couple tangled in time, drugged
by blood, shedding years like hair on the flowered rug.

This is the place where peace grows
like a green frond set among waters aerial
with dragonflies. Where, at noon,
the trees section the broad falling
leaf of light, and space color upon the millpond,
yet do not move because motion
might be lost upon silence.

This is the place where a stone,
given its occasional career, could disturb
little with an arc and fall,
for the pond would swallow all voice
and shrug circling ripples into its banks until
moss had absorbed this small wet gift,
showing a fancy darker.

This is the place where one may
abet his heart's romance, deceiving his eyes by
unconsciously confusing
slow change with no change. But even
here, dream makes way for declensions of wind and sun.
The alders will grow, moss will dry.
Wings will pulsate, then plummet.

This is the place where peace rests
like ferns beyond lilies. The trick is to wear it
as a mantle, but to know
cloaks for cloaks, shelters for shelters.
Beneath this revery of surfaces, fish wait
for the dragonfly's mistake. The
trick is to lose, but to own.

THE WELL

He and his go to the spring, have gone
to the same old well, through the weeds in the yard,
under the oak arching its limbs over
their heads — for water have gone, to drink
from the welling rock in the four seasons,
though good liquid has long sprung from the pipes in

the kitchen, the clocks' hands are now turned
by sparked wire; the grandchildren's dolls no longer
are chipped off the old block stowed in the wood
shed, near the willow wands. Still he goes.
Why? Time, measured by the golden rule, the
honey vine suckled in the sun inching day

by day over his canopy of
firm timbers — those hours are over now. He knows
no age reclaims another. But the well
is deep and old. Its tunnel strikes through
stone: strata which buoy up all things and all
men: himself, his — whoever thirsts in this world.

SCHOOL DRAWING

There is a road: no
one is walking there. Brown
paper, black paper triangles
wrangle with the air
to make a windmill

striping a crayon
sun. A black arrow points
away from the blades that turn in
fire. It is burning,
and there is no wind.

An Ordinary Evening in Cleveland

I

Just so it goes: the day, the night —
what have you. There is no one on TV;
shadows in the tube, in the street.
In the telephone there are echoes and mumblings,
the buzz of hours falling thru wires.

And hollow socks stumbling across
the ceiling send plaster dust sifting down
hourglass walls. Felix the cat has
been drawn on retinas with a pencil of light.
I wait grey, small in my cranny,

for the cardboard tiger on the
kitchen table to snap me, shredded, from
the bowl.

II

Over the trestle go
the steel beetles grappled tooth-and-tail — over and
over and over there smokestacks

lung tall hawkers into the sky's
spittoon. The street has a black tongue: do you
hear him, Mistress Alley, wooing
you with stones? There are phantoms in that roof's trousers;
they kick the wind. The moon, on a

ladder, is directing traffic
now. You can hardly hear his whistle. The
        oculist's jeep wears horn rim wind
shields; the motor wears wires on its overhead valves —
        grow weary, weary, sad siren,

        you old whore. It's time to retire.

III
The wail of the child in the next room quails
        like a silverfish caught in a
thread. It is quiet now. The child's sigh rises to
        flap with a cormorant's grace through

        the limbo of one lamp and a
slide-viewer in your fingers: I cannot
        get thin enough for light to shine
my color in your eyes; there is no frame but this for
        the gathering of the clan. Words

        will stale the air. Come, gather up
our voices in the silent butler and
        pour them into the ashcan of
love. Look, my nostrils are dual flues; my ears are
        the city dump; my eyes are the

        very soul of trash; my bitter
tongue tastes like gasoline in a ragged
        alley.

IV

The child cries again. Sounds
rise by the riverflats like smoke or mist in time's
bayou. We are sewn within seines

of our own being, thrown into
menaces floating in shadows, taken
without volition like silver
fish in an undertow down the river, down time
and smog of evenings.

V

The child cries.

VI
Do you hear the voice made of wire?
Do you hear the child swallowed by carpets,
the alley eating the city,
rustling newsprint in the street begging moonlight with
a tin cup and a blindman's cane?

VII
The lamps are rheumy in these tar
avenues. Can you sense the droppings of
flesh falling between walls falling,
the burrowings of nerves in a cupboard of cans?
Can you hear the roar of the mouse?

VIII
There is nothing but the doorway
sighing; here there is nothing but the wind
swinging on its hinges, a fly
dusty with silence and the house on its back buzzing
with chimneys, walking on the sky

like a blind man eating fish in an empty room.

The Old Professor and the Sphinx

It is a dry word in a dry book
drying out my ear. I squat and swallow
my tongue here in this chair,
the desert of my desk, summer bare, spreading
like a brown horizon into regions grown arid
with erudition. A caravan of books treks

stolidly across my eyes while I,
the Sphinx, a phoenix nesting in my skull,
pry into inkwells and
gluepots seeking the universal solvent.
There is none. The pages as I turn them sound like sand
rattling in the sec temples of a beast gone to

earth with the sun. I lie caught in my
creaking dune, shifting with the wind of the
pharaohs, wondering if,
somewhere, I have not missed my valley. Upon
the walls of my office there are Oriental prints
hanging stiff as papyrus, whispering their brown

images into the silent air.
I know the poems on my shelves speak with
one another in an
ancient language I have somehow forgotten.
If there is rainfall, I recall, the desert blossoms —
but I have somewhere lost the natural prayer

and instinctual rites of the blood
which can conjure clouds in seasons of drought.
There is but ritual
remaining; no honey is in the lion's
hide; my temples have mumbled to ruin: they endure
disuse and despair. An archaeologist of

cabinets and drawers, I exhume
paperclip skeletons, the artifacts
of millennia: red
ballpoint pens with nothing in their veins, pencils
like broken scimitars, notebook citadels empty
of citizens — the crusader has squandered his

talents on bawds, grown hoary in their
service. The town is sacked: the bawds are gone
to tame younger legions.
Look into my sarcophagus: the tapes are
sunken over my hollow sockets. Slowly the waste
swallows my oasis like a froth of spittle.

The well of holy heaven has gone sec;
the sun begins its famous dance of wives.
Freres and handmaidens, come sip the blue from
aster's eye: pudgee and peewee liking
from free fields, milkweed stealing gold from gourd
and globe. In a word the world wags. Singing
vines take husbands from the hearth, settle them
among the clods and clouds where meadows waste.

The apple of the daisy knows it's true:
the earth is, after all, a world, though tan-
tamount to tangerines — equal in worth
to a curlew's call, a cell of bees in
amber comb, the curl of water, welter
of the summertide sunning autumn's falls.

OLD NEWS

"Six weeks gone," the doctor said,
that odd good luck look walking his lips along

the trail blazed by the tip of
his tongue. "Six weeks gone, son. She'll be fine. Lousy

in bed, though," shaking his head.
"You'll be used to the idea come daylight,"

and off he went, his eyes propped
wide with a good call's work — blasé, not quite bored

by the old wonder with which
I was left: the old bride whose acquiescence,

I now find, can swallow down
this house with its carpet silences; stillness

of pillows; the couch couching.
Outdoors, the dark lies in the hollows of trees.

Night descends like a muffled
lamp. These eyes seize on ancient things: the roadway

sleeping between its curbs, the
lurking swell of a still flat belly, and the

lidded moon risen, unwinking, on the world.

Hundreds of yards of woodland
smashed and torn.
They had been a long while dying,
these great beasts;
one, of a broken neck — the lucky
one. Thirst took
the other: even on his side he'd dug
a dozen

holes, deep as his hooves could delve,
trying for
water. It had been one of those
tremendous
agonies. There lie the two moose still,
locked upon
love's combat, horns fused. All is as it was.
The bulls are

dead; so says the placard hung
upon the
glass; thus they were found, silent in
the forest.
The point and object of contention
had long since
vanished when men happened upon these hulks
steaming in

a spring thaw. But it was not
love that had
conquered; as usual, it was
time. Engrossed
with death's petrified grove and with the
heart's beasts calm
in the wildwood, we stand frozen by love's
passing glance
reflected in the forest beyond the glass.

He touched the switch
and lit his burning bush,
then waited for a voice
to come chiming,
green as ever, from among

its needles. He
listened hard, but the spheres
made no music of their
colors, and the
angel sitting on top of

everything just
sat there holding a bulb.
Maybe it was the wires:
he checked them, but
could find no short anywhere —

all the lights were
tight in their sockets; no
cane's cellophane was caught
in anything
electrical. The angel

was shedding spun
glass hair everywhere, but
glass is no conductor.
He sat and he
waited. The dark windows flashed

back the light of
his burning bush. The house
hummed with sleep, with couches
stolid as cows
chewing carpet cuds. Comfort

bleated in dim
corners void of any
echo. Once, the furnace
rumbled under
him like a tame inferno:

for a moment
he thought that the bush had
started to speak. At last
he gave up, turned
off the angel and its lights.

In the darkness
his bush loomed against the
window through which cold stars
came stabbing out
of a wind he had not heard,

nor wished to hear.
Snow lay trackless in his
yard, but at his panes some
sound, like fingers
touching for purchase or for

entry, moved and
scratched, scratched on the frost-etched
glass. Open! said the wind;
wings battered his
door. Trembling, he tried the lock

and went to bed.

In a drawer he found
a clock, its cord wound
among some chessmen, its crystal
broken and its digits gone dark with
dust. It needed

a spark to set it
going upon its
rounds. It would mutter some constant
monotone among queens and knights. Pawns
could listen as

they lay tumbled in
a grove of fallen
rooks: it was love's visage he saw
rising from the floor on which he stood.
She was blind to

the careful mating
moves, her blunt palms like
inexorable whispers at
his ankles, her numbers obscuring
the chequered field.

It is now ten minutes after midnight,
December 5th, 1965. In honor
of the attack by the Japanese
on Pearl Harbor, Hawaii, on
December 7th, 1941, all channels

are running movies about war. On one
channel, the come-on is newsreel footage of the
bombing inserted into a film
made by the Japanese. Channel
9 has topped that: also Japanese, the movie is

science-fiction: the Third World War is just
beginning. I'll take a gangster film — Channel 3:
it sounds incredible, but the third
world war is already over
over here. This one is American. Let me check

the *T. V. Guide*: " 'Five.' (1951).
The only five survivors of atomic war
revive man's ancient hostilities
and prejudices." The whole thing
is starting again. So I have turned to writing this

poem as I watch. I have survived one
Armageddon; I shall build a microcosm.
I am writing very carefully:
the woman is pregnant, and the
Negro is building a house. I want my facts to be

accurate, in case this is the last thing
to be left. The sounds do not matter, only the
sense. If you are reading this, I hope
that it will not upset you, sir,
whoever you are. It may be that my typewriter

was hocked, passed peacefully from dark shelf to
dark shelf in ancient shops until it was sold for
scrap. Grant us this: that was possible.
But if you should find this lying
rolled in my machine, the letters of our alphabet

scrambled in the dust, grant us this much more:
we foresaw the end too clearly for it to matter.

THE GIRL FROM THE GOLDEN WEST
for Diane

He was on a pale horse when he came
   riding out of the dark East,
      the manuscript of
         a novel,

beery and dogeared, under one arm,
   and a shotgun strapped to the
      saddle. You thought you
         were supposed

to be his heroine — the girl with
   long hair, from The Golden West.
      You knew your role to
         the last dot

on the last page. And you were ready.
   The plot had to do with love
      and fidelity —
         yours, of course.

You knew he'd be true to nothing but
   art, its imitation of
      life: you were to be
         his living

imitation of love. He would write
you down under the long wind
out of the mountains;
your pages

would fall like leaves into the big white
winter of the world. It would
be a grand book,
a Western.

So when he came riding out of the
East, you were prepared, even
though he did not look
his part: his

beard, for instance, reminded you of
Hemingway's rather than
Odysseus's.
But, after

all, you were hardly Helen yourself,
only a plump girl of woods
and weather out of
Cooper's verge.

So when he came you took the gun
and wrote the last flourish. It
was not love, though, was
it? It was

only your revenge upon his art
at last, and you were not his
book, but only a
scant chapter.

And that's why the horse bearing you out
through the sunset is pale, not
sable, and that's why
we are blue,

not stricken in the wind from the West.

The fire is eating
the paper. The child who drowned
is burned. Asia is in flames.
    As he signs his great
bill, a minister of state chars

    at the edges and curls
into smoke. The page rises,
glowing, over our neighbor's
    roof. In the kitchens
clocks turn, pages turn like grey wings,

    slowly, over armchairs.
Another child drowns, a bill
is signed, and the pen blackens.
    The smoke of Asia
drifts among the neighbors like mist.

It is a good day for burning.
The fire is eating the news.

Desire today is a cavern of snow;
  ice rimes all limbs with synonyms for wind.
    Yesternoon it was goat-time, time for horns
      rampant on a field *vert* under the woods
        quartered in a southern compass. Toucan
          tones rose close beneath the surface of shade,

        threatening rupture. Poet, draw your shade
today upon a mirror made of snow
    shadowed. Men may hibernate if bears can.
  Desire must sleep in a cavern of wind
    till it may be harried awake by wood-
    pecker beak and Pan's sunsharp or ramshorns —

    Too many words, like girdles built of horn,
      confined in an attic. How to say *shade*
    but make it mean more, as: tiles of the wood
laid for light to walk on; and to have *snow*
imply more than God's linoleum. Wind
    is wind, but direction matters. Who can

    help me? Where's my muse today? Shake your can,
  you errant Echo, and get home. My horns
sprout long as the cuckoo's song while you wind
    your own clock and make love with your own shade
someplace up a cavern or down the snow
    where wild Narcissus buds among your woods.

The forest of my seasons grows strange woods
sometimes; this fall of words grows as it can,
not as it ought. My pen is cold as snow:
its ink runs like chilled honey from the horns
of silence. Lie you down, lie down in shade,
word-warbler. Sleep sound with your mistress wind.

And while you sleep, dream. Dream of the south wind
needling you awake with slivers of woods:
birch and pine, maple that sweetens in shade;
oak on the white hillside. Dream, if you can,
of grey moles, brown mice, winter's hunting horns
blown to silence. Dream no longer of snow,

for time and flesh shall do more than wind can
to blend your words with woodwinds and woodshorns.
There will be tonics. It's time for shades now.

Nor was it the moon,
appointed, pure in outline,
    huge among stars, painted;
    nor was it the wind.

Chinese firecrackers,
Chinese lanterns; O the flare
    and the pop! Acres of
    summer went well with

    the fields of light made
by the moon tugging at tides.
    And the gale mewled offshore.
    You could hear the hiss

    of rockets. The hiss of
the flames on the beach. The
    surf's hiss too, the kiss of
    sand. It was not the

    moon. Nor was it the
    old wind offshore, moaning.
It was partly these, partly
    their white permanence

    and cold. But it was
    the pop too, the flare, the
flash of flame. Short. Slight. Red and
    unappointed. The

scrim of those quick, quaint
with life. The scream of bright
rockets; night's backdrop; summer's
curtain. Clams in a

bucket. Fire them, shell
them in the summer dark.
A heap of shells on the shore
looks like the moon's shards.

As you stand there, Melora, winking at
     my world (doubly obscured by the
          curtain's mist) your eye is
a sparrow flung searching among the morning
trees. Your gaze floats, windreft, inquiring
     for its sulking mate. But it

     is all to no effect, for she will not
          rise from her nest for sheer pique at
               weathervanes which would spin
my wet kind of world today, not your sunny
one. So the braver eye flies homeward.
     Not until you turn toward

          hallways and cupboards do you unwink. Those
          two brown birds address their ire at
               me. Yes, I'm to blame. My
wings are only knuckles now; my mind is prey
to weasels and martens, and winds are
     merely the rustlers of nests.

SCARECROW
for 'Dolph

We pumpkins worship you. We orange globes,
harrowed in youth, hollow in our old age,
aspire to your straw. In the darkness
of our swelling and decay, in our days
of rook pestilence and the owl's blight
which scampers among the vines we spin in
furrows and the furbelows of weed, we
do you homage. All honor, Scarecrow! You
there, sunstruck, eminent among us, rag
lord of moonlight, crucified among stars,
sighted as none of us may be. The world
in which we root unrolls unendingly
beneath your gaze, furlongs your province.
We pumpkins worship you, we orange globes.

*I cannot see. Buttons for eyes, what would
I see? If I could hear, the crows' whispers
could tell me only of some simple fields,
potato-eyed and corn-eared, extending
to limits that would only barb my sleeve
and rend my cloth, if I could walk to them.
You worship me? a pole for a spine, a
timber for my extended bone, fingers
of hay stolen by wrens? I bleach and shake,
I shudder in the moon's dark. Pumpkins, crowd
of orange globes, I whistle in the wind.*

Scarecrow, we too would whistle in the wind.

My raceway of sheets last night became
a cool trotter, unwinding with grace. Today,
autumn peeps imponderably out of
the soggy drought July had posted
on the foothills. It is August

here in Saratoga; the races
open tomorrow. Yesterday a filly
worked out her own odds, snapping two of her
ankles while we watched. She was done in
by a green syringe. She lounged on

the turf, staring from one farthest eye,
both her forehooves angled like ballerina
slippers. With her, summer has staggered: it,
too, soon will drop and the jockey sun
grow grey above the world's brown hide.

✿　　✿　　✿　　✿　　✿

When a thoroughbred loses its
pins, there's no more running. Snort if you
will, but reason, too, exhausts itself when
cause falters. Men have run down when barred from the
race. Summer is a fragile courser

here in the North; our racers are
all imports from the southland. Summer
will not slow for falling leaves, nor haul our
sleighs: it will linger, pawing its reluctance
to leave, but its strength is of only

short will, meant for one swift effort.
Watch the summer run its oval, it's
a winner now — nothing can stop it! The
stands urge their encouragement upon open
air; shouts fall and rise like the fall wind

that moves out of the foothills now, sure,
pervasive, wild.
Blooded summer shies.

I have always wanted to write
a poem about a
pumpkin. It is one of those
impossible subjects. You know
the feeling, left over from childhood's

fantasies of what childhood is
like. Come the Indian
summer of any year, 'mums
and trees burning their clean
colors into the air, one thinks of

all seasons, past and future, but
particularly of
the pumpkin, Ceres' good Jack,
grinning his candlepower in-
to the scarecrow's menace. Northern spies

engage in autumnal intrigue;
winesaps hit the local
cider mills, and there's a witch
in every stook.
Cozy, but the
real spice lies with that vandal made of

air, the empty ghost our scarecrows
cannot frighten. August:
the field is a tangle of
sunlight wound in vines, covered with
pillows of foliage. Blossoms flare

briefly, then fall. Green nodes take their
place, begin to swell. Then,
the infant pumpkins seem to
disappear. The patch is a great
green whirligig of tendril and vine.

One night, only the moon watching,
magic occurs. The dawn
finds the bright globes lying in
windrows, clinging to tangles of
brown twine. Next, even the vines crumble

into film. We take October's
flesh and make it grin. We
set it in our window to
frighten shadows with a hollow shell,
but wind seeps in, and the flame wavers.

It is a dawn quick as swallows
    peeling to shear through peals belled
from the lone town steeple. Autumn
falls from green heat like a chestnut felled
out of its prickly jacket. An only

    jay walks in the pines. A cone of
        cold sweeps chill's needles soughing
    through the day's screen doors. There can be
    no cushioning today: to wake
shall be a sharp thing. The person on his

    private ticking will be palsied
        from his sheets; his numeral
    be rung, the coils of consciousness
    spring him into good, woollen light,
without armament, to meet himself in

    mirrors and still halls. Meet himself:
        find his blood walking a thin
    line, alarums unsleeping him.
    Brazen as flame leaving ash for
the sere elm's leaf, Autumn will have settled

    into summer's pallet — patchwork
        and quilting: that poor thread of
    dreams curling at the doorsill. It
    is done, the keen tone spoken, wrung
out of the bronze tongue of silence. Winter;

allcolor; whiteness. Who will braid
    our years now into what skein
of circles? Bells fail in the streets;
the hall empties us into ice,
sheeted, sheer as mirrors, unreflecting.

Like a fleet thief, this sparrow has
stolen stillness. He keeps it in a
purse of bones. The aperture in which he
quit quickening is thin: an airy dimness
between our house and its false shutter.

Here's a sparrow that couldn't fall.
I cannot even pry him loose. The
shutter has been stunned with bolts; the wall won't
drop its trophy. For certain, bird, you did not
fly diving into quiet. It is

your tail that caught you up and will
not let you down. How in heaven did
you back to your demise? This December
sky seems somewhat grimmer for your defection.
The overcast will not be cast off.

*   *   *   *   *

So this small absence is noted and
duly recorded. His mate impatiently
waits near the crack into which he crept for
warmth. It will be a cold day elsewhere,
my lady, before this midwest

wind hovers about his flight again.
One feather works loose. It falls. The overcast
is cued: a flake has launched an avalanche.
My sympathy is for both your songs,
but less for the live, for at least

(for all and any hurt a sparrow
feels) when winter learns to thaw there's always spring.
Death will shrink to due proportion: a bird's
eye view of a worm, perhaps. But right
now, be vigilant with your grief,

wife. Snow is vital too. It sucks what
warmth was left today when wings hung fire.

53

In this season light
is equivocal. The moon
    rises too early.
She is the eye of the ghost

of the shadow of a world.
    She is gravid bone.
Her dust settles the season
    beneath her lumen.
We will take frostlight if we

must in lieu of blind wicking.
    The moon is an urn
burning ice and umbra. Stars
    have seeded her. Now
in season her time has come.

It will be soon our bones say.

THE SNOW DEVIL

The wind is telling rumors
to the snow; the snow listens
and takes common counsel. Drift

and drift, they bury silence
at the root of a pine which
stands forth from the forest. The

woods brandish green spears and will
not turn a cone to listen
to sophistry. The single

pine stands for all, roots sunken
in the proper element.
Snow and wind will challenge, raise

a cold champion to stand
against the pine. The wind gives
breath to frost: crystals rise in

spirals and plumes: it is a
snow devil glittering in
armored currents. The pine is

engaged, but briefly. A small
storm glistens through its boughs. At
its base silence is buried

further in a thin white rain of
mail. Nothing is finished.
The green woods wait in the wind.

The greenwood waits in the wind.

THE STROLLER

A stick strolling with an old man. Trees
messy with spring: woodland a squander
of roots. The road had nowhere to go,
so it stayed flat and listened closely
to the tap, tap of the runaway
stick. It was spring roundabout, and it
was springtime straightway.
                              "Come, sing me songs
of death," said the old man to the sun
nearly black in his eyes. But the most
his sun would do was roust out a flock
of sparrows to swivel in the air.

"Drop in my ears sounds of worms turning
the sheets of my bed —" but the earthworms
lengthened quietly underneath moist
shadows, and quietly contracted.

"Let me hear nails driven in hard oak,"
the old man whispered to his stick. But
the cane stuttered on stones just then, made
no word out of the good green light.
                                      "Just
as I feared," the old man muttered, "there
is noplace to go when winter is
over."
       And the road stopped when he stopped.

ABOUT THE AUTHOR

LEWIS TURCO has been reaching a growing audience with his poems since 1959. In addition to publication in the leading journals, his poems have appeared in a number of distinguished anthologies and in two collections besides the present volume: *First Poems*, a 1960 selection of The Book Club for Poetry, and *The Sketches*, 1962 winner of the American Weave Chapbook Award. Mr. Turco's *The Book of Forms: A Handbook of Poetics* was published by E. P. Dutton & Co. in 1968.

Mr. Turco has ventured toward new forms of expression in his collaborations with workers in other arts. A series of poem-prints resulted from his work with the printmaker Thom Seawell, and a chamber opera "The Dark Man," written with the Dutch composer Walter Hekster, is nearing completion. The poem "November 22, 1963," which is included in the present publication, has been widely reprinted in this country and translated abroad; it serves as the basis for a ballet, "While the Spider Slept," choreographed by Brian Macdonald, Director of the Royal Swedish Ballet, and performed in Stockholm. It is also in the repertoire of the Royal Winnepeg Ballet in Canada.

Mr. Turco is Associate Professor of English at the State University College at Oswego, New York.